# CINQUAIN POEMS

BY LISA M. BOLT SIMONS

ILLUSTRATED BY KATHLEEN PETELINSEK

**The Child's World®**

Published by The Child's World®
1980 Lookout Drive · Mankato, MN 56003-1705
800-599-READ · www.childsworld.com

ACKNOWLEDGMENTS
The Child's World®: Mary Berendes, Publishing Director
Red Line Editorial: Editorial direction
The Design Lab: Design and production

Photographs ©: Andrew Olney/Thinkstock, 4; Goodshoot/
Thinkstock, 12; John Foxx/Thinkstock, 17

ISBN 9781631436932
LCCN 2014945440

Printed in the United States of America
Mankato, MN
November, 2014
PA02240

## About the Author

Lisa M. Bolt Simons is a writer and a teacher. She has published more than ten books for children. She has also been awarded grants and awards for her writing. Besides writing, teaching has been her passion for 20 years. She lives in Minnesota with her husband and boy/girl twin teenagers. Her Web site is *www.lisamboltsimons.com.*

## About the Illustrator

Kathleen Petelinsek is a graphic designer and illustrator. She has been designing and illustrating books for children for 20 years. She lives in Minnesota with her husband, two dogs, a cat, and three fancy chickens.

# TABLE OF CONTENTS

# What Is a Poem?

What do songs, nursery rhymes, and greeting cards have in common? They all use poetry! Poetry is a special type of writing. Poems often use lines instead

*Many greeting cards have short poems inside.*

of sentences. Lines do not have to be complete thoughts. Sometimes a line has only one word.

How words sound in poetry is important. Poets pay attention to the length of words. They also pay attention to **syllables**. These are the parts that make up a word. Clapping along as you say a word can help you count its syllables. For example, *frog* has one clap or syllable. *Spi-der* has two syllables.

frog

spi-der

IN-sect

ga-ZELLE

A syllable can be **stressed**. This means it is said slightly louder than the other syllables. Other syllables are unstressed. They are said more softly. The first syllable is stressed in *IN-sect*. The second syllable is stressed in *ga-ZELLE*. The pattern of stressed and unstressed syllables helps create a poem's rhythm.

Poets choose their words carefully. They try to write poems that create images in readers' heads. To do this, a poet often includes descriptive words. These words can create powerful images.

A poet does not always say exactly what is happening in the poem. Sometimes, the reader must guess what a poem is about. The images in a poem help the reader guess the poem's meaning.

# WHAT IS A CINQUAIN?

A cinquain (pronounced SIN-cane) is a short poem with a few rules. All cinquains have five lines. Cinquains were probably first written in France in the 1000s AD. Some cinquains were **stanzas**, or parts, of longer poems. These cinquains often had **rhyme**. Words that rhyme have the same ending sounds. *Pig* and *dig* rhyme.

Rhymes in poetry often have a pattern. This pattern is known as a poem's **rhyme scheme**. Letters of the alphabet are assigned to the different rhymes in the poem, starting with A. In a poem with an ABABB rhyme scheme, the first and third lines rhyme. The second, fourth, and fifth lines share a different rhyme. Cinquains were once written in the rhyme schemes ABABB, ABAAB, or ABCCB.

Summer means *flowers* **A**
Grass growing *green*, **B**
Storms that bring *showers* **A**
To wash and *clean*, **B**
But don't forget *sunscreen*! **B**

**?**

How could you rewrite this cinquain
to use an ABAAB rhyme scheme?

CHAPTER TWO

# 2

# Syllable Patterns

Most cinquains written today don't rhyme. They use a syllable pattern instead. This means each line has a certain number of syllables.

American poet Adelaide Crapsey created the cinquain syllable pattern in the early 1900s. Most cinquains still use this syllable pattern. Crapsey's pattern is 2-4-6-8-2. The first line has 2 syllables. The second line has 4 syllables. Line has 6 syllables. And line four has 8 syllables. Finally, the fifth line has 2 syllables again. Crapsey based her pattern on a type of Japanese poem called a haiku. Haikus have 17 syllables in three lines.

Recess

Ladders and slides

Monkey bars that stretch arms

Swings, ropes, poles, and
   laughing children...

Stop, rain!

| | |
|---|---|
| | **2 SYLLABLES** |
| | **4 SYLLABLES** |
| | **6 SYLLABLES** |
| | **8 SYLLABLES** |
| | **2 SYLLABLES** |

**?**

What is happening in this cinquain?

# CHOOSING YOUR WORDS

It can be challenging to pick words with the right number of syllables for your cinquain. With only five lines, these poems are very short. That means poets must choose their words carefully. They should pick words that create strong images in readers' minds.

*Colors can help create strong images. Think about the words that describe the different colors of the rainbow. Red and green have one syllable. Or-ange and yel-low have two syllables. In-di-go has three syllables!*

Another way poets create strong images in a cinquain is by using action words. These are words that describe an action. *Sing*, *jump*, *dance*, and *tickle* are action words. "She is in gymnastics" doesn't create a strong image. "She flips, jumps, and twists" is a more interesting line. It creates a stronger image in a reader's mind.

Tumble
twist, jump, bend, leap.
Techniques of gymnastics
that make me fit and strong but tire
me out.

? Which action words do you find in this poem?

Words that **appeal** to the five senses also help create strong images in poems. The five senses include sight, smell, taste, sound, and touch. Poets try to be as specific as possible when appealing to senses. Instead of saying a flower "smells sweet," a poet could say the flower "smells like pink cotton candy." What are some other ways you could describe a sweet smell?

CHAPTER THREE

3

# Telling a Story

Cinquains can be about anything. Poets can write cinquains that describe something, such as the way a tiger looks.

*What is your favorite story? Write a cinquain
using the characters from that story.*

One of the poems in Chapter 2 describes recess. It talks about objects you might see on a school playground.

Another way to write a cinquain is to write a very short story. Stories have a beginning, middle, and an end. Cinquains that tell stories must also have these elements. Stories also have at least one character. This is the person, animal, or object the story is about.

Most stories also have a setting. This is the place where the story takes place. Poets try to make sure story cinquains have strong images that help describe the setting. They use action words and description words. These help readers picture the story and where it takes place.

One way to think of strong words is to imagine answers to question words. These are *who, what, where, when, why,* and *how.* Where is the best place to have a picnic? Who is a funny person? What is

a crayon made of? Your answers will help you pick interesting words to use in your cinquains.

Poets often find surprising ways to end their cinquains. They use words readers might not expect for the final two syllables. They can be the conclusion to the story. Sometimes the end is funny. Sometimes it gives away a secret about the poem. Other times, a poet will sum up the whole poem.

Soapy
circle all soaked,
I hold the stick and blow
so patiently, and then it won't—
It did.

**?**

What is the surprise ending of this cinquain?

# NOW IT'S YOUR TURN!

Cinquains give poets a chance to express ideas in interesting ways. Because cinquains are so short, poets need to think hard about the words they choose. Now that you know how to write a cinquain, it's time to write your own! You can write a cinquain about anything. What will you write about?

# TIPS FOR YOUNG POETS

1. Practice clapping out syllables to different words. Try *cup, penny, vegetable, calculator,* and *refrigerator*. How many syllables does each word have?

2. It's OK to break rules in poetry.

3. Write a story cinquain about an activity you did today. Make sure to include a beginning, middle, and an end.

4. Focus on specific words that another poet may not think of. Instead of writing *vegetable*, write *Brussels sprouts*.

5. Read your cinquains out loud.

6. Keep working on your cinquains, even after they are written. Try switching out some of the words for more interesting ones.

7. Try to end a cinquain with a surprise or something unexpected for the reader.

8. Read lots of poems, and read all different kinds of poems. Reading poems will make you a better poet!

# GLOSSARY

**appeal (uh-PEEL):** To appeal is to suggest or encourage something. Poets often appeal to the five senses in cinquains.

**haiku (HYE-koo):** A haiku is a short Japanese poem that has 17 syllables in three lines. The first line of a haiku has five syllables, the second has seven syllables, and the last line has five syllables again.

**rhyme (RIME):** Words that rhyme have the same ending sound. The words *plant* and *slant* rhyme.

**rhyme scheme (RIME SKEEM):** The pattern of rhymes in a poem is its rhyme scheme. Cinquains were once written with a rhyme scheme.

**stanzas (STAN-zuhz):** Stanzas are groups of two or more lines in a poem. Some cinquains were once stanzas of longer poems.

**stressed (STREST):** A word or syllable is stressed when it is said a bit stronger or louder than another word or syllable. The pattern of stressed and unstressed sounds decides a poem's rhythm.

**syllables (SIL-uh-buhlz):** Syllables are units of sounds in a word. You can tell how many syllables are in a word by clapping your hands as you say the word.

# TO LEARN MORE

## BOOKS

Janeczko, Paul. B., ed. *Firefly July: A Year of Very Short Poems*. Cambridge, MA: Candlewick Press, 2014.

Salas, Laura Purdie. *Bookspeak! Poems about Books*. New York: Clarion Books, 2011.

Singer, Marilyn. *A Strange Place to Call Home: The World's Most Dangerous Habitats & the Animals That Call Them Home*. San Francisco: Chronicle Books, 2012.

## ON THE WEB

Visit our Web site for lots of links about cinquains:
www.childsworld.com/links

*Note to Parents, Teachers, and Librarians: We routinely check our Web links to make sure they're safe, active sites—so encourage your readers to check them out!*

# INDEX